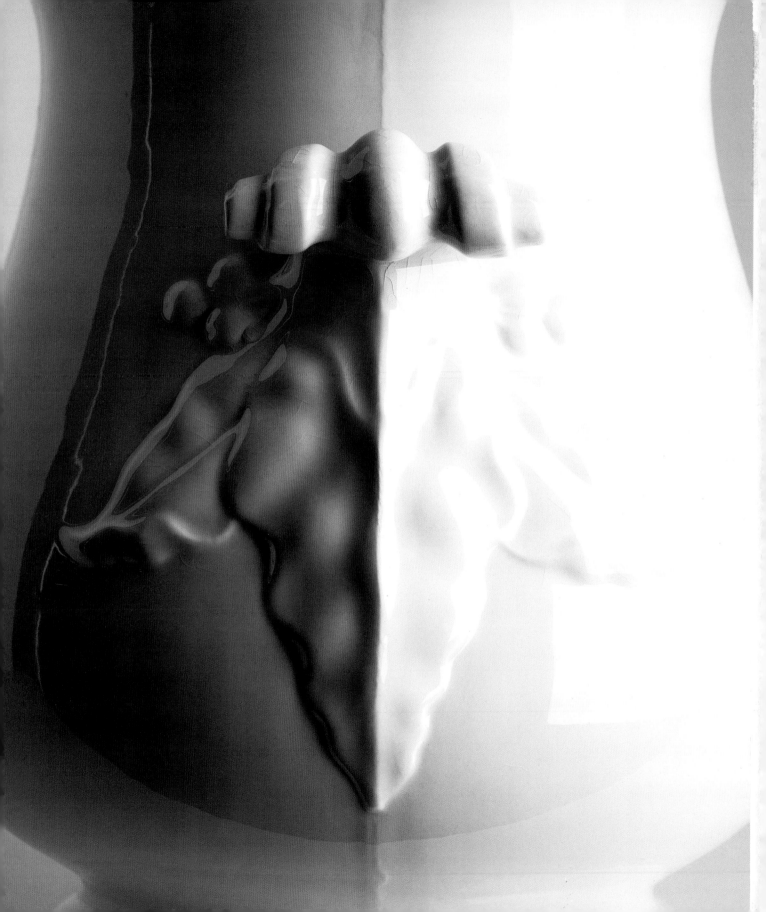

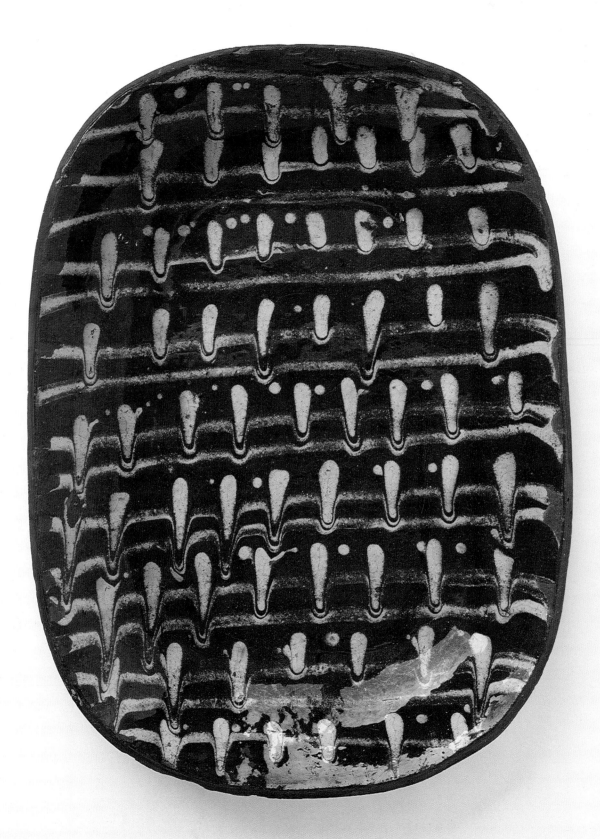

EVERYDAY THINGS™

KITCHEN CERAMICS

SUZANNE SLESIN

DANIEL ROZENSZTROCH

STAFFORD CLIFF

LOCATION PHOTOGRAPHS:
MARIE-PIERRE MOREL

STUDIO PHOTOGRAPHS: MARC SCHWARTZ

DESIGN: STAFFORD CLIFF

ABBEVILLE PRESS
PUBLISHERS

NEW YORK • LONDON • PARIS

Editor: Jacqueline Decter
Art Director: Patricia Fabricant
Production Editor: Owen Dugan
Production Manager: Lou Bilka
Production Artwork: Matt Sarraf

First edition
2 4 6 8 10 9 7 5 3 1

Jacket front: American yellowware bowls with green glaze date from between 1900 and 1930 (see also page 141).
Jacket back: Quart-capacity creamware and pearlware mugs were popular in the early nineteenth century (see also pages 124–25).
Endpapers: Detail of a slip-decorated redware platter, early nineteenth century.
Facing half-title page: Detail of ironstone water jar in the Maddock Pear pattern shows its plain body and elegant handle.
Frontispiece: An English early-nineteenth-century slip-decorated loaf dish, measuring 14 x 21 in. (35.6 x 53.3 cm), is rare because of its large size.
Pages 3 and 4: Ironstone platters in a particular pattern often ranged in length from 10 to 20 inches (25.4 to 50.8 cm).

Library of Congress Cataloging-in-Publication Data
Slesin, Suzanne.
Kitchen ceramics / Suzanne Slesin, Daniel Rozensztroch, Stafford Cliff ; location photographs, Marie-Pierre Morel ; studio photographs, Marc Schwartz ; design, Stafford Cliff.
p.   cm. — (Everyday things)
Includes bibliographical references and index.
ISBN 0-7892-0288-3
1. Kitchen utensils. 2. Ceramic tableware. I. Rozensztroch, Daniel.. II. Cliff, Stafford.
III. Title. IV. Series.
TX656.S59   1997
642'.7—dc21   97-9410

PREFACE

Our search into the world of kitchen ceramics began with the most ordinary of everyday objects: the bowl. Plain, serviceable basic mixing bowls, the mainstays of so many kitchens of generations past, kept catching our eyes at flea markets. There were yellowware ones and ironstone ones, some with bands of color, some embossed with friendly scenes, all appealingly innocent and comforting.

Once used only for mixing cookie, cake, or waffle batter, the bowl began to take on different functions in our daily lives. It would often emerge from the kitchen to grace the table, metamorphosed into a bowl for serving salad or pasta. And in its smaller sizes, the bowl came in handy for soups or breakfast cereals. Soon our enthusiasm for ever-different varieties and our attempts to put together nesting sets led to more bowls than we could possibly use. Some inevitably cracked, and although no longer suitable for serving food, they were so beautiful in our eyes that they deserved to be put on display.

In time we became fascinated by the different techniques used for and shapes of what we considered to be everyday pottery. For us, ironstone was the most elegant; redware, an extraordinary example of folk art; yellowware, the most universally appreciated; and mochaware and spongeware, seductive in the range and variety of their imaginative decorations.

These once ordinary things opened our minds to the importance of kitchens and dining rooms in the everyday life of the past. Setting a beautiful table, sensing the warmth that accompanies the preparation of food in the kitchen, and enjoying a feeling of conviviality are but some of the basic pleasures embodied in these everyday objects. We also happen to be a part of a generation that is trying to redefine the ways in which it lives and entertains.

We may appreciate and love many things from the past, but we have had to find a more informal, stylish, and timely way to use them today, so we have learned to move yellowware out of the kitchen and into the dining room; to place a slip-decorated loaf pan on the hall table; to set a party table with mismatched cut-sponge plates; or to line the mantelpiece with a series of graphic mochaware mugs; and we are not afraid to arrange a bouquet in a huge ironstone milk pitcher. In so doing, we not only appreciate the timeless forms of this well-loved pottery but realize in how many ways vintage kitchen ceramics have helped us rediscover an art of living for today.

PRECEDING PAGES A slip-decorated redware loaf pan commemorates the alliance between Lafayette and Washington at the time of the American Revolutionary War.

LEFT The embossed pale beige surface of these vintage yellowware bowls, which are part of a nesting set, has a strange textural affinity to old golf balls.

LEFT Pieces of rough-hewn Portuguese spongeware take on a contemporary look when stacked ready to be used in a high-tech kitchen.

RIGHT A French plate from Forges-les-Eaux has the octagonal shape that was popular in the middle of the nineteenth century and a raised, beaded border painted in brown spatterware. It is outlined in a circle of manganese, and the central floral motif was painted by hand.

HISTORY

rom the end of the seventeenth century and well into the nineteenth, the Staffordshire region in central England—an area not far from the busy port of Liverpool that became known as The Potteries—supplied a large part of the ceramics (ware made of clay or fusible stone) used in England and exported all over the world. Plentiful coal and numerous rivers with beds from which clay could be conveniently culled made the region attractive both to new manufacturers and to the potters and other workers who were to produce the thousands and thousands of items.

Ironstone was only one of the many kinds of ceramics that evolved, but because of its plain, utilitarian nature, it quickly became very important in the daily life of the burgeoning middle class. In America, where early colonists did not bother with many of the niceties of their English ancestors, wares such as the inexpensive ironstone grew quickly in popularity, replacing the rough redware they had used before. Tables set with clean, white dishes were in favor, even in rural households. Ironstone pieces, whether imported from England or made in America, were touted as being important "for health's sake," as they were easy to clean thoroughly. American potteries flourished in the late 1870s, not only because of the plentiful clay deposits needed to make ironstone but because of the presence of potters who had emigrated from England.

In the case of spatterware and spongeware in particular, different countries, including Holland, Germany, and Belgium, started developing their own factories to protect themselves from the influx of British-made wares. Many young English potters traveled to France, settled there, and became closely associated with well-known French manufacturers to whom they had given their expertise and experience. The best known of the potters in Staffordshire was Josiah Wedgwood, who had noted that the expansion of the export market could become far more important than the market in his native country.

Until well into the twentieth century, simple yellowware or spongeware cooking and serving utensils were basic necessities in almost every household. Heavy yellowware bowls, with their decorations of colored bands, were used daily for mixing batters and holding dough. Milk was poured into sponged pitchers, and slope-sided pie plates were constantly in transit between the stove and the table. Fresh food was preserved by drying, salting, pickling, and smoking and kept in all kinds of ceramic storage crocks.

The durability of kitchenwares was important, as many families had limited incomes and enough room to store only a few things. Kitchen ceramics would continue to be thought of as the mainstays of every household until industrialized glass and plastics became popular with the arrival of electricity and the modern icebox.

LEFT A stoneware crock decorated with a cobalt blue parrot, made between 1859 and 1870 by F. B. Norton of Worcester, Massachusetts, would have originally had a wooden lid that fitted inside the crock and rested on the contents.

In America the kitchen, with its large-as-possible fireplace, was the center of the house. It was used around the clock for preparing and serving meals and for preserving food. In the early nineteenth century molded ceramics began to replace pewter cooking utensils. By the end of the century, yellowware items of all kinds were widely available by catalog.

Kitchen ceramics, from the most rustic of wares—the redware loaf pans and storage jars of Colonial kitchens—to the ironstone that defined the tastes and aspirations of the Victorian middle class and the ubiquitous sturdy, serviceable yellow-ware bowls and canister sets, all serve as a link between the home-spun values of the old-fashioned kitchen and the emergence of the modern household.

TOP LEFT Potters at work in one of the numerous ceramics factories in southwestern France.

BOTTOM LEFT Alfred Meakin's Royal Albert Works in Tunstall, England, at the turn of the century.

RIGHT Tall enamel kilns tower above the Royal Albert Works.

TOP Two of Alfred Meakin's workers mix raw clay amid the complex system of belts and pulleys that drive the machinery.

BOTTOM Saggars—the clay pots that serve as protective casings for pieces while they are being fired— are filled with glazed wares prior to the firing.

TOP Workers place clay wares in silicon sand inside the saggars before putting them into the bisque oven.

BOTTOM To ensure safe export all over the world, finished wares are protected with straw and packed inside large wooden crates.

It took many people to staff a turn-of-the-century English country house ktichen. The large number of ceramic dishes needed every day fill a rack in one of the kitchen's many rooms.

IRONSTONE

hite ironstone, called white granite by ceramic historians, came into its own in the 1840s in England. Potteries were centered in the Staffordshire area because of its rich natural resources and proximity to the bustling port of Liverpool. From there the sculptural molded wares could be shipped to the growing markets, especially in America.

Patented in 1813 by Charles Mason, English ironstone pieces were originally decorated with transfer-printed designs in blue and mulberry. But it was the embossed, white-glazed versions that found the largest markets in the New World. From the 1850s to the 1870s, plain white ironstone, inexpensive because it was undecorated, and available in hundreds of patterns to satisfy a demanding new clientele, became the rage. By midcentury even the poorest rural families had replaced their redware household items with pieces of white ironstone. And because of its weight and solidity, ironstone proved sturdy enough to be packed for travel at a time when pioneering families were moving west.

Bluish white in color, the glazed earthenware pottery had heft and withstood high temperatures, making it particularly useful in brewing tea, that mainstay of English life. Ironstone reached its zenith of design in the hands of such master potters as Thomas, John, and Joseph Mayer, three brothers who founded the T. J. & J. Mayer pottery in 1837 and would create some of ironstone's most assertive body shapes and memorable finial and handle designs.

Many of the earliest designs were often variations of the Gothic style, with hexagonal and octagonal panels that gave the overscale serving pieces a majestic, powerful look. In the 1860s softer naturalistic motifs such as berries and wheat were popular and in the course of the decade evolved into elaborate floral and leaf-decorated designs. By the end of the 1870s, simpler, more geometric shapes had replaced the more ornate forms of the earlier decades.

In mid-nineteenth-century America white ironstone came to be known as farmer's or thresher's china, a reference to its modest beginnings. By the end of the century, plain ironstone was no longer in favor for the table. The growing urban middle class preferred more formal, richer-looking, and more ornate table settings.

Even though there are many pieces of ironstone that are considered rare today, the extraordinary production that found its way to America in the second half of the nineteenth century makes collecting a variety of ironstone still possible. White ironstone has proved adaptable to a modern lifestyle, not only because it can withstand daily use but also because it is dishwasher-safe. Collectors may covet the most elaborate designs, but in an era when simplicity is prized above all, the basic, classic, and timeless forms of many vintage white ironstone pieces lend them a quintessentially modern feel.

LEFT Gleaming white quintessentially English ironstone soup and sauce tureens are satisfyingly solid yet have the elegant look of fine china. T. J. & J. Mayer's mid-nineteenth-century Classic Gothic pattern has crown finials and sculptural handles that contrast with the simple geometric lines of the main bodies of its serving pieces.

Tureens, made throughout the second half of the nineteenth century, were used primarily for serving vegetables and featured lids for keeping food warm. In oval, hexagonal, or octagonal shapes, and often available in three

sizes, they matched the more elaborate serving pieces in their patterns.
Most were designed with handles for convenience. Special attention was
often paid to the finials and handles.

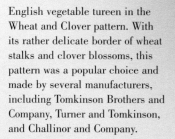

English vegetable tureen in the Wheat and Clover pattern. With its rather delicate border of wheat stalks and clover blossoms, this pattern was a popular choice and made by several manufacturers, including Tomkinson Brothers and Company, Turner and Tomkinson, and Challinor and Company.

RIGHT Oval gravy or sauce tureen and matching platter, in the Scrolled Bubble pattern, created by the J. W. Pankhurst company. It can still be used for its original purpose even without its matching ladle.

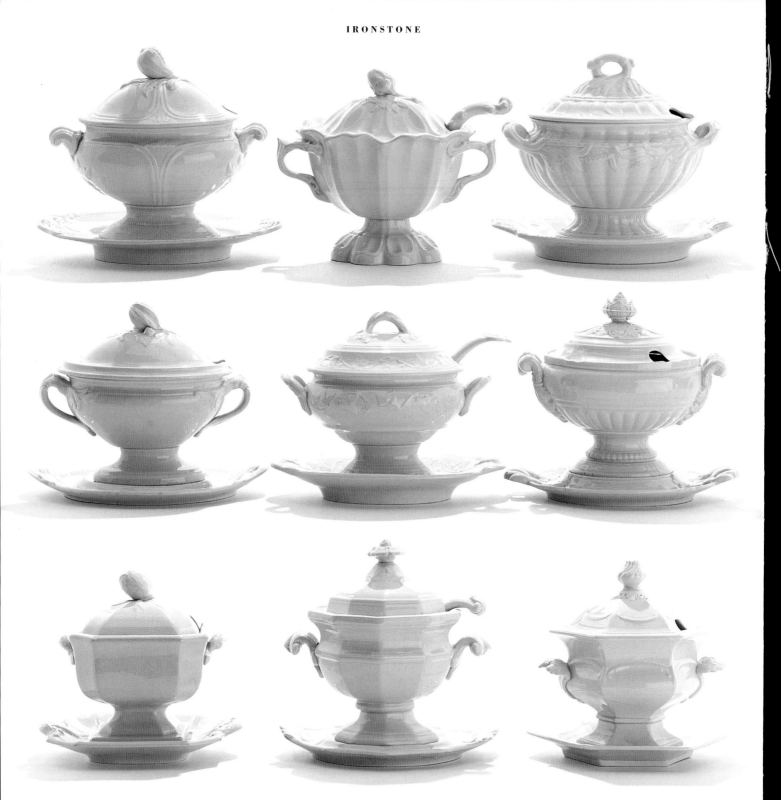

A complete sauce tureen consisted of four pieces: a lid, a base or bowl, a liner, and a ladle.
In most cases the holes in the lid accommodated the ladle for a right-handed person. The tureen
at the far right, second row, has a spoon slot made for a left-handed person. The six-sided tureen,
bottom row, third from left, in the Sydenham pattern, has a more transparent-looking glaze.

The Ribbed Raspberry tureen, top row, third from left, is intricately decorated with ribs of varying lengths on which raspberries and leaves are superimposed. J. & G. Meakin was one of the makers of this classical pattern. Gelson Brothers' tureen, second row, third from right, with its handle of interlocking birds' beaks, is rare. The pattern is called Eagle Dove, Diamond, or Thumbprint.

BELOW AND RIGHT Different in size but identical in design, the soup and
sauce tureens on matching platters were made by T. J. & J. Mayer, in two
patterns registered in 1847. The Long Octagon, below, has distinctive
cushion-shaped finials. The Classic Octagon pattern, right, has finials in
an acanthus-leaf motif and scrolled handles.

Made by various English potters in
the 1860s, including T. & R. Boote,
Burgess & Goddard, and William
Adams & Sons, and originally used
solely for serving fruit or compote,
these graceful footed bowls, shown
on the rough-hewn pantry shelves
of a country kitchen, are easily
integrated into any contemporary
table setting.

Pedestaled serving pieces came in a wide variety of heights and shapes. The shallow ones, top row, were for serving cookies, the deeper ones for more formal fare. Some had reticulated, or cut-out, bowls that not only were decorative but allowed air to flow around fresh fruit or still-warm roasted chestnuts.

An elegant piece, in which flowers could be arranged, might be placed in
the center of the table or on a sideboard. Often the serving pieces matched
the design of the dinner service.

ABOVE A T. & R. Boote syllabub (from "sillery," a wine, and "bub" for bubbly) bowl, above, dating from 1851. Wine was poured into the vessel, which was then placed under a cow for milking. The resulting beverage was foamy and did not need additional beating. The bowl was also used for serving hot toddies. The beverages were ladled into small cups with handles, top.

RIGHT A 3½-inch (8.9 cm)-high cup, in the Gothic pattern, originally used for syllabub. Today it makes a perfect espresso cup.

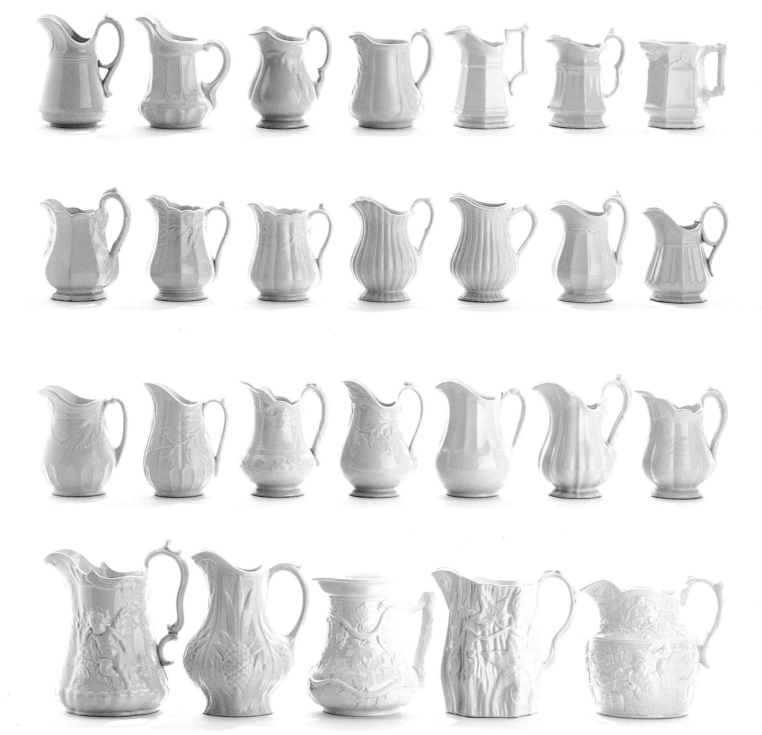

Most ironstone makers produced a set of seven, or sometimes eight, pitchers for each of their patterns. The two largest were water ewers for washbasins, bottom row; the next two sizes were for serving water or milk at the table, second and

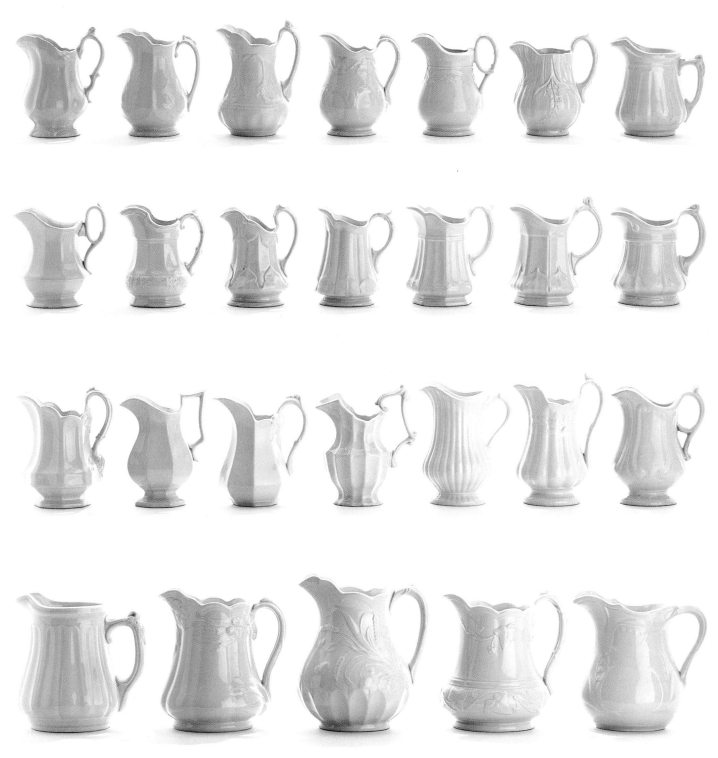

third rows; and the three smallest were creamers that matched teapots, coffee pots, and sugar bowls, top row. The large water pitchers were often decorated with naturalistic, beautifully detailed allover designs.

ABOVE Tea, coffee, and other hot beverages were each assigned their own serving pieces. English Gothic-style pitchers and a lidded hot-chocolate pot reflect the mid-nineteenth century's new tastes.

RIGHT A voluptuously shaped pitcher from the 1850s has a broad spout and graceful handle that is a continuation of the body. Today it has found its place on a console as a stylish vase.

A hundred years ago, tea drinking in England was nearly an all-day affair. There was breakfast tea, "elevenses"—the British version of the 11 A.M. coffee break—afternoon tea, and high tea, or supper. So, it was not surprising to find so many different kinds of teapots. Typically a tea set included the teapot, a creamer, a sugar bowl, a waste bowl for tea leaves, and handleless cups with deep saucers.

The teapot's body, spout, handle, and lid and its finial were sometimes molded separately. English potters began exporting the sturdy teapots to America in the 1840s. The country's changing tastes in architectural and decorative styles, from the Gothic Revival patterns of midcentury to the floral Victorian motifs of the latter part of the century, are reflected in the teapots' patterns.

LEFT An English or American heavy-lidded cheese keep, 13 inches (33 cm) tall but of heroic proportions, is decorated with raised dogwood branches, vines, grass, and wildflowers. Similar cheese keeps were meant to be painted and covered with a majolica glaze.

ABOVE Ironstone was also made into utilitarian kitchen equipment such as molds for jelly, pudding, and blancmange—a milk pudding sweetened with cornstarch. The thick, heavy material resisted very hot liquids.

TOP ROW In America especially, syrup pitchers with pewter or tin lids
were used to serve a dark syrup the color of molasses, which was known as
long sweetening.
MIDDLE ROW Gravy boats were a necessary accessory when roasted meat

or poultry was served. Some designs mimicked early Greek patterns, and the handle shapes matched the details on the large dinnerware sets.
BOTTOM ROW Butter dishes often came in two sizes and included an etched liner that separated the butter from the ice used to keep it chilled.

TOP LEFT A T. J. & J. Mayer well-and-tree platter was designed for serving roasted meats. The juices would flow from the swirled branch-like indentations to the deep well. Heavy legs supported the 20-inch (50.8 cm)-long platter.

BOTTOM LEFT A complete set of seven stacking platters in the Sydenham pattern range in size from 10 to 20 inches (25.4 to 50.8 cm) long.

RIGHT A Victorian undertray for a hot chestnut basket has a gently undulating, pierced rim. The reticulated pieces of ironstone were formed in molds and then cut out by hand with a penknife to achieve the lacy effect.

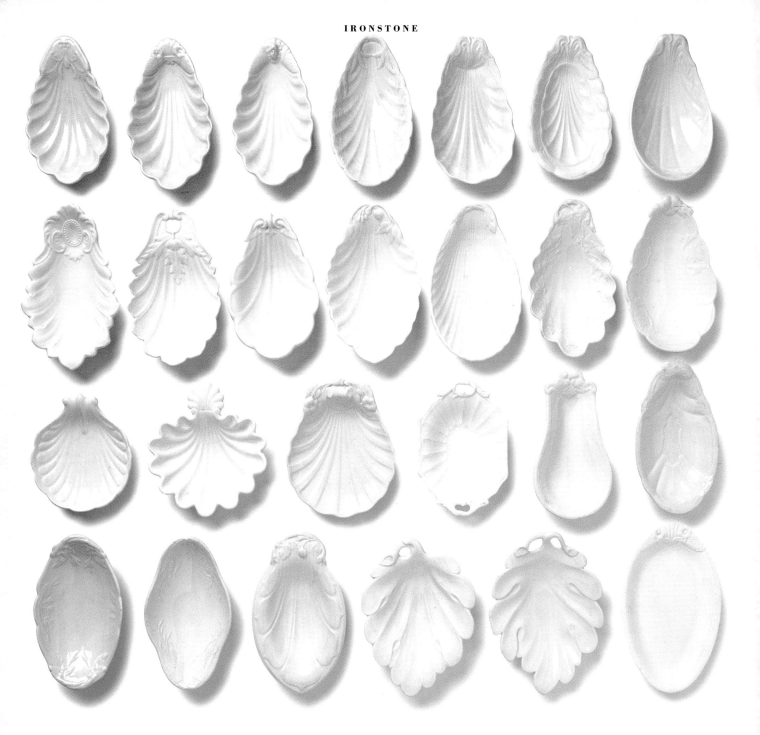

ABOVE English meat and fish dishes were traditionally served with a wide variety of pickles, chutneys, and relishes. The handlelike decorations on one or both ends of the relish dishes made them easier to pass around the table. The designs incorporated the major motifs of the different ironstone patterns. Leaf and shell shapes were particular favorites.

RIGHT This elegant relish dish makes its appearance these days at the cocktail hour.

A collection of more than four hundred pieces in the President Shape pattern by John Edwards of Fenton, registered in 1855 and again in 1856, gives an indication of what a complete service of ironstone once encompassed. Unusual is the complete set of eight graduated pitchers. Now kept on the open shelves of a dresser in a country kitchen in Connecticut, the pieces are put to everyday use.

ABOVE Dinner plates came in seven sizes, the largest having a diameter of 10¹/₂ or 11 inches (26.7 or 27.9 cm). Available in every pattern that was manufactured, the plates had wells of varying depths and decorated rims. There was traditionally no decoration where food was placed.

RIGHT Today often bought one by one, ironstone plates in different patterns can be used to set a modern informal table. Their sturdy clay bodies and thick glazes make them dishwasher-safe.

REDWARE

Redware, the first pottery produced in quantity in Colonial America, had as its base the ubiquitous red clay that was used for making flowerpots, bricks, and a host of other household objects. Once tin and glass became more common for making such wares as candlesticks, frames, and mugs, the redware potter came to specialize in pitchers, storage and preservation jars, and platters.

Redware potters molded the clay by hand or on a foot-powered potter's wheel and became adept at the application of slip, a clay solution that had the consistency of buttermilk and was applied to the clay body with a slip cup. The slip-decorated item—with its wavy lines, names, or everyday sayings—was then fired in a kiln to make the design permanent. The techniques of making redware did not change; thus, a redware platter made in the mid-eighteenth century is similar to one made seventy-five years later. Potters rarely marked their work, and it is often hard to distinguish between American and European pieces. Not surprisingly, given the patterns of immigration, German examples resemble redware pieces crafted in Pennsylvania.

The slip decorations offered the potter freedom of expression. It was common practice to order customized designs for special occasions. Names were popular, as was an early American form of advertising, encouraging customers to drink in taverns or visit people in ill health.

The fragile quality of the clay and the poisonous nature of the lead glaze led to redware's eventual replacement after the mid-nineteenth century by other types of inexpensive ceramics. Today, the fragility and the unusual textured surfaces of many redware objects have made them rare collector's pieces. Redware platters, plates, and bowls are appreciated for their graphic and calligraphic designs, as well as for their bold geometric patterns. No longer the serviceable wares of Colonial America, they are now unique pieces, worthy of being displayed as folk art.

LEFT Redware objects, such as these nineteenth-century pitchers and mugs, were relatively simple to make and were useful additions to the pewter pitchers and plates and the wooden bowls found in nearly every American household.

ABOVE AND RIGHT Two lavishly decorated slipware platters, crafted in
Pennsylvania about 1825.

Slipware plates from Long Island, New York, Connecticut, and Pennsylvania display the variety of imaginative patterns potters obtained using the slip technique. After being slip-decorated, the dishes were fired in a kiln, a process that made the liquid-looking designs permanent. The slip, which had the consistency of buttermilk, was made from a pale yellow clay that came from England.

ABOVE Loaf dishes have the wavy lines and orange-red background typical of slip-decorated redware. The oval shape is unusual, however.

RIGHT This very large slipware loaf dish was probably made on Cape Cod about 1800. Today it is a rare piece, serving a decorative function rather than a utilitarian one.

LEFT Loaf dishes were often decorated with slipware designs that commemorated historical events. The pan at the top, for instance, was made in honor of General Lafayette's visit to America during the American Revolutionary War.

RIGHT Slip was often applied in flowing script to decorate the red clay bodies of plates with their owners' names, sayings, or descriptions of the food they were intended to hold or advertise, such as "Chicken Potpie" and "Lemon Pie." The plates were made as special orders for specific people or to commemorate events.

stylized flower and leaf decorations. The straight-sided shapes and flaring necks, as seen in the pitcher second from the right in the bottom row, are typical of Eberly pottery. The brown-and-green splash patterns contrast with the yellow ground.

ABOVE Jugs and storage jars, all dating from the first quarter of the nineteenth century, were made in Massachusetts, New Hampshire, and Maine. Some were used for storing molasses and vinegar, top row; others, for keeping herbs. The jars with lids and handles were also sometimes used as stew pots.

RIGHT Storage jars with manganese glaze over orange glaze came from New England. The one on the left on the top shelf was made in Hartford, Connecticut; the one on the right, in Maine. The jar on the bottom shelf was made in Massachusetts in the early nineteenth century.

Rare examples of slip-decorated
bowls, from 7¾ inches (19.7 cm)
to 13 inches (33 cm) in diameter,
with brightly colored geometric
designs, were crafted in Hagerstown,
Maryland, in the period from 1790
to 1820.

SPONGEWARE

Spongeware is characterized by the technique used to decorate it rather than by the material out of which it was made. It is widely thought to be a descendant of spatterware, pottery decorated by a technique that first appeared in the Staffordshire area in the second half of the eighteenth century. Spatterware decoration involved the application with a fine brush of hundreds of dots to form colorful borders or overall designs. Spongeware gets its name from the small cut sponges with which color was applied (although bits of cloth, potato stamps, and brushes were also used). It was a faster, more efficient method of decorating than spatterware.

An early master of spongeware, Thomas Whieldon (1719–1795) of Little Fenton, Staffordshire, developed such sophisticated techniques that his name has become the generic term for the dense spattering of brown, yellow, and dark green that distinguished his glazed wares. Whieldon was inspired by the look of tortoiseshell, agate, and richly veined marble. Some of his followers eventually traveled to France to work at such ceramics centers as Forges-les-Eaux, Sarreguemines, and Luneville, where they shared the secrets of their techniques. Maastricht, the Netherlands; the Saar Basin in Germany, where pottery was sometimes marked "Villeroy and Boch"; and Tournay in Belgium also became important centers for spatterware and spongeware manufacturing.

By the mid-nineteenth century wares were being exported in huge quantities to the Far East, West Africa, South America, and North America. W. Adams & Sons of Stoke was an important English producer; in the 1860s he was reputedly producing some 70,000 dozen pieces a week for foreign markets. But most pieces were not marked, in part because they were considered quite ordinary.

By the turn of the century spongeware production was well assimilated into American ceramics manufacturing. Red Wing, Minnesota, and East Liverpool, Ohio, were important early centers.

Spongeware designs were applied to a wide variety of ceramics, the most common being stoneware and yellowware objects. Manufacturers described their method as "mottled." A related technique known as cut-sponge, in which simple designs such as stars, crosses, flowers, and geometric motifs were applied with stamps cut from potatoes, was well known in the nineteenth century in Ireland and Scotland. This work was often done by children on ordinary dishes and sometimes even on marred pieces to camouflage imperfections.

So many pieces of spatterware and spongeware were produced up until the 1930s that it is surprising how rare they are today. Thanks to the early and widespread exportation of spongeware, it now turns up in far-flung places and can be discovered in both flea markets and fancy antiques shops all over Europe, the United States, and even Asia.

LEFT Sponging techniques unite a Portuguese pitcher and a Russian bowl.

Using a cut-sponge technique that has also been called stick-spatter or stick-sponge, these English dinner plates and soup bowls were decorated with geometric and floral motifs, including the popular camellia border.

These soup bowls are part of the recently salvaged cargo of the *Adgillus*, a sailing ship that was built in Quebec in 1873 for Thomas Harrison of Liverpool. On its maiden voyage in October 1874 the ship encountered a heavy squall some eighteen miles off the Lancashire coast. The crew threw the cargo overboard and just managed to abandon ship before the vessel went down.

LEFT Two monochromatic soup bowls made in Holland at the end of the nineteenth century and decorated in the cut-sponge technique have the same elephant motif in the center but different styles of borders. They were destined to be exported to Indonesia, then a Dutch colony.

RIGHT Plates and bowls from France, England, Scotland, Wales, and Belgium display a variety of cut-sponge or potato-sponge designs, ranging from simple borders to complex overall patterns.

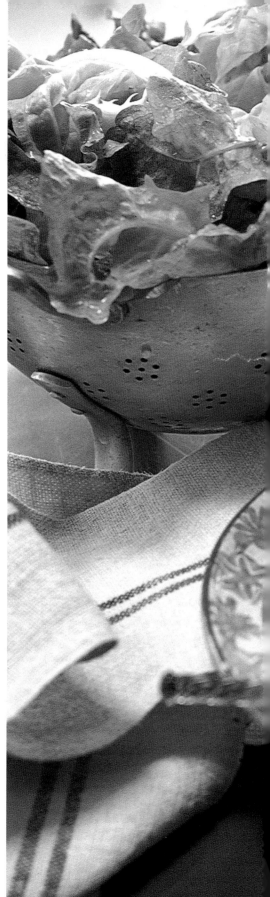

ABOVE Oval spongeware baking or serving dishes are similar to those made by the Mayer Pottery Company of Beaver Falls, Pennsylvania, in the early 1880s.

RIGHT A bowl with a pink cut-sponge rim was made in the early twentieth century at the Kuznetsov factory in St. Petersburg, Russia.

ABOVE The shape of these basic bowls is typically French. Traditionally used for café au lait at breakfast time, they were made in huge quantities and various sizes by most of the ceramics manufacturers throughout the nineteenth century. Because they were such ordinary items, many were not even marked with the name of the producer. The oldest are from Creil-Montereau: top row, third and fourth from left; second row, the two center bowls; and third row, second from left.

RIGHT An English mid-nineteenth-century cup that had lost its saucer has been felicitously paired with another saucer in a similar hue. The small bowl—its shape is known as custard—now serves as a sugar bowl.

ABOVE Nineteenth-century English and American handleless teacups were also widely used in Europe for drinking consommé. The one at the top is in the Amish Snowflake pattern and is considered "flowed" because of the seepage of the blue color into the body of the cup.

RIGHT Overlapping saucers have been separated from their matching cups. It is rare to find intact cup and saucer sets.

LEFT English water and milk pitchers have charming spongeware decorations. The pattern on the pitcher in the top row, right, is called Arno; it was made by the Willets Manufacturing Company in Trenton, New Jersey.

RIGHT In Normandy, a region of France known for its apples, there is a tradition of drinking cider from a special kind of cup.

ABOVE AND RIGHT Brightly colored Portuguese dinner plates and oval dishes, flat and shallow, and of different sizes, were originally very ordinary and produced for sale at country fairs in the early twentieth century. The glazed terra-cotta bodies on which the spongeware designs were applied were made in Coimbra, a ceramics center in Portugal.

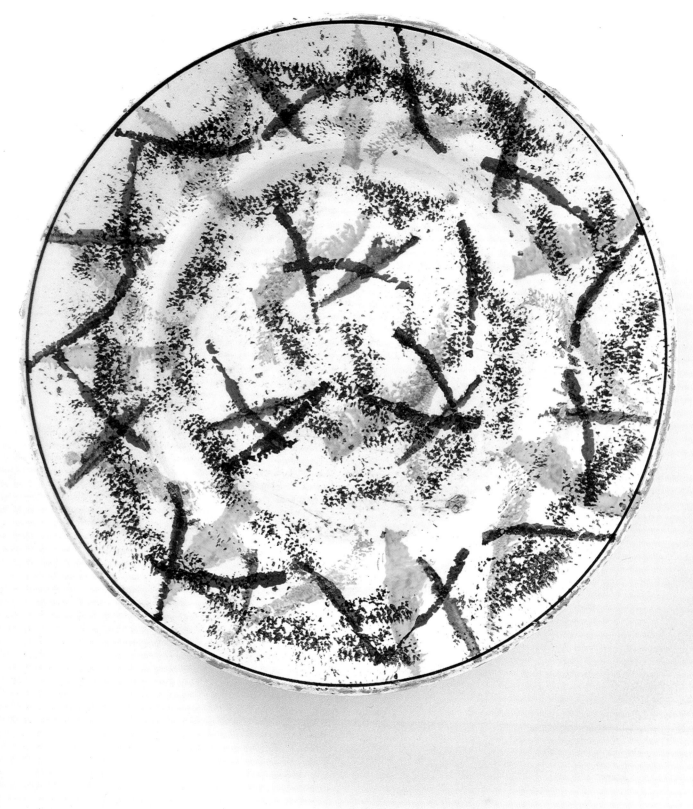

ABOVE Similar in shape, small Portuguese glazed terra-cotta bowls display variations on a roughly executed spongeware design.

RIGHT Turn-of-the-century bowl and plates from Portugal have an unusual random design.

ABOVE AND RIGHT Miniature French soup tureens, bowls, plates, and platters were made as girls' toys at the turn of the century. They were produced in the same shapes and patterns as full-scale dinnerware sets by the same manufacturers.

Two nineteenth-century 9-inch (22.9-cm) plates made in Ferrara, Italy,
were meant to be displayed proudly on the shelves of the family china
cabinet. The border was decorated in spongeware, and the central motif,
here of a woman smoking and of a bearded man, was painted by hand.

LEFT AND RIGHT
Decorative plates, dating
from the mid-nineteenth
to the early twentieth
century, were intended
to be hung on walls or
placed on the shelves
of china cupboards. The
hand-painted or stenciled
central motifs, such as
landscapes, houses,
people, flowers, and
animals, were often
framed with spongeware
borders. The rooster,
a traditional symbol of
France, was a popular
subject.

LEFT Dishes displaying
similar overall spatterware
and spongeware designs
were made at different
times in different places.
The left-hand pieces in
the top and bottom rows
are late-eighteenth-century
Staffordshire creamware
chargers by Thomas
Whieldon of Little Fenton.
They show this master
craftsman's high-quality
glazes and richly colored
spongeware surfaces.
Whieldon was extremely
influential, and his name
became synonymous with
this type of pottery. A few
decades later, a generation
of potters traveled from
England to France, where
they introduced their
spongeware and glazing
techniques. The right-
hand piece in the center
row is mid-nineteenth-
century French. The other
three are late-nineteenth-
century Portuguese.

RIGHT Three French
chargers manufactured at
Forges-les-Eaux in the
mid-nineteenth century
have a circle of manganese
that contrasts with the
overall spongeware design.
They take on a modern
allure when incorporated
into an informal table
setting in a Paris loft.

PRECEDING PAGES, RIGHT, AND OVERLEAF
Blue-sponged pitchers—tall ones for water and
round-sided or bulbous-bodied ones usually
used for milk—are the most popular forms of
spongeware. Pitchers were for the most part cast
in molds from coarse stoneware clay, then fitted
with different handles and spouts. The overall
patterns were achieved by dabbing colors—in
these cases blue hues—onto the surface of the
pitchers with sponges, brushes, or bits of fabric.
The technique, born in England, was widely
adopted in the United States, where it continued
until 1930. There was a seemingly infinite variety
of patterns, from the overlapping circles of a
chicken-wire-like design to horizontal or vertical
stripes, sometimes adorned with floral motifs.

ABOVE AND RIGHT Spongeware storage containers, especially butter crocks, were a mainstay of the kitchen pantry before iceboxes and then electric refrigerators made some of them obsolete. Later versions of tea and salt containers were probably part of canister sets.

SPONGEWARE

Spongeware's sturdy shapes made it ideal for everyday kitchen use. Water coolers, also known as kegs (bottom row, third from the left), were sometimes equipped with a filtration system and are the ancestors of the modern office water fountain. Covered casseroles without handles, used for baking as well as serving; baking dishes, cooking crocks, and stew pans with wire bail handles for manageability; mixing bowls of various sizes; and bean pots (bottom row, third and fourth from right) were ubiquitous in the turn-of-the-century American kitchen.

OVERLEAF Once strictly utilitarian, a spongeware teapot, custard cup, and pitcher have become part of the decor on the mantelpiece of an eighteenth-century farmhouse in Connecticut.

Antique platters and plates with
bright blue spongeware designs
are rare. Serving dishes often had
scalloped edges, and square or oval
shallow bowls came in a variety of
sizes. In the last quarter of the
nineteenth century the production
of these wares was centered in
Maryland and New Jersey.

An ambitious collection of blue-and-white spongeware, including dinner plates, cups and saucers, soup bowls, pitchers, and platters, is still put to use when the table is set in the dining room of an old farmhouse. A paneled, glass-doored dresser has been painted a matching dark blue to provide a perfect background for the dishes.

MOCHAWARE

he term *mochaware* comes from two kinds of stone that were shipped in large quantities from Arabia to London in the late eighteenth century through the port of Mocha on the Red Sea. The stones—one was mocha stone, the other moss agate, a semiprecious stone used in jewelry—revealed when cut distinctive dendritic, or treelike, patterns. Originally, only earthenware slip-decorated with dendritic patterns was known as mocha. A hundred and twenty-five years later, mochaware was the name given to earthenware with all sorts of colored slip decoration.

The earliest mochaware with slip decoration, combed marbling, and many other effects was made in England about 1770. The objects were first thrown on a wheel, then put on a lathe and turned to remove any excess clay. Textured bands were sometimes applied, and while the slip was still wet the characteristic dendritic designs were achieved by dotting the upside-down vessels with a few drops of a tobacco infusion or urine. Chemical reaction and gravity created the treelike motifs.

Staffordshire and Yorkshire were the British centers for the production of mochaware, with many of the pieces made especially for export to America. France also produced mochaware in quantity, and the French manufacturers were known to hire English pottery workers who were experts in the field, in the hope that they might divulge their trade secrets.

Archaeological finds from early-nineteenth-century America place mochaware in middle- and lower-class households, an indication that these ceramics were originally inexpensive. Shards have even been found around the slave quarters and elsewhere at Monticello, the home of Thomas Jefferson. Given that each piece of mochaware one sees today looks unique, it is hard to believe that these wares were produced in enormous quantities in England, France, and also later in America. But because mochaware objects were used every day in kitchens, pubs, and inns, relatively few pieces have survived unbroken.

Today we look at these graphically innovative objects with a different eye, seeing in them designs that predate—often by two hundred years—modern art movements such as op art and abstract expressionism.

A typically French eighteenth-century faience coffeepot, marked "Sarreguemines," is shown with a group of slightly later British pieces, including mugs. All are slip-decorated with dendritic, or treelike, patterns resembling the markings of moss agate.

English mochaware jugs dating between 1800 and 1830 include a rare early-nineteenth-century yellow-bodied example, far left. The white-bodied jugs are either creamware or pearlware. The dendritic decorations were produced by letting a few drops of a colored acidic solution containing urine fall onto the wet slip-coated surface of the jug before it was fired and glazed.

White-bodied creamware and pearlware jugs display an array of decorative slip surfaces that were applied as the vessel revolved on a horizontal lathe. The geometric designs were achieved mechanically on an engine-powered lathe; the other ornamentation was done by hand, with the slip oozing through goose quills, in a technique similar to that of icing a cake. The round motifs, called cat's-eyes, were attained by using a special cup with three separate compartments for the three different colors of slip.

TOP Early-nineteenth-century oversize jugs, measuring between 9 and 10 inches (22.9 and 25.4 cm) tall, have a combination of twig, wave, cat's-eye, and earthworm decorations. The tin handles are replacements.
BOTTOM An extremely rare glazed earthenware double jug, probably meant for carrying water, was made in England about 1830.

RIGHT An elaborately decorated English creamware jug, made about 1775, is at home on an early American mantelpiece. The slip-marbled jug is encircled by raised garlands and bands that have been brushed with a copper oxide glaze to produce a brilliant green hue.

ABOVE Creamware, pearlware, yellowware, and drab-bodied jugs date from the eighteenth century, with the exception of the largest, which was made in the mid-nineteenth century. Its shape is similar to that of pieces made in Derbyshire and later in America, and its surface is composed of tiny bits of clay in different colors that were rolled smooth on a large sheet before being applied to the surface, using wet slip as a glue.

RIGHT While nineteenth-century pubs often served beer in mochaware half-pint or sometimes quart tankards, these days the tall mugs are more likely to be used to hold tea or coffee.

In the early nineteenth century quart-capacity creamware and pearlware mugs were popular in homes and pubs throughout the northeastern United States. The shape of these mugs lends itself particularly well to all manner of geometric and patterned decorations. The earliest example, dating from about 1770, is the third from the right in the bottom row.

LEFT A small mochaware mug is decorated with a geometric pattern in manganese on a cream background.

RIGHT Detail of an earthenware bowl, the inside of which is slip-decorated in a cable motif.

Open salt containers, top row, and mustard pots with lids date from the early nineteenth century. The technique employed to decorate the pot at the far left in the bottom row is called rouletting. It entails running a tool similar to a pie crimper through the pliable clay, filling the recesses with black slip, and then shaving away the excess.

TOP A 7-inch (17.8 cm)-diameter English bowl was made about 1820 and decorated with cat's-eye and cable motifs. The cable was achieved by continuously overlapping the cat's-eye design. Known as the London shape, this bowl style, which began to be made about 1810, replaced the eighteenth-century Chinese-style round-sided bowls.

BOTTOM The knob and handles of this covered bowl, made in England

about 1830, are spattered with cobalt. It was found at a country auction in Wisconsin.

OVERLEAF At Eastfield Village in upstate New York, a large bowl, left, was recently crafted by Don Carpentier, a collector and ceramicist who specializes in early American techniques. The original slip-decorating techniques, as seen in the bowl on the right, were used to create the new design.

BELOW AND RIGHT Collectors refer to the unusual decoration shown on these nineteenth-century pieces as palmate, lollipop, balloon, or tobacco leaf, while scholars call it dipped fan, referring to the way it was achieved: a shallow vessel would be filled with slip, then other colors of slip would be dripped on the surface, in stripes or randomly. The piece was then dipped into the rainbow-hued pool and held straight up until the slip settled. The method would be repeated several times around the pot's circumference. The teapot is by John Shorthose, who worked in Hanley, Staffordshire, from 1807 to 1823.

Collectors refer to
these little shakers
as peppers or pepper
pots, even though
museum curators like
to call them castors.
They date from about
1800 to 1860.

YELLOWWARE

lain, utilitarian, and durable yellowware was the most inexpensive and basic of kitchen ceramics. Its name derives from the clay from which it is made, which varies in hue from pale yellow to light brown. The clay is baked at high temperatures before being covered with a clear alkaline glaze. Yellowware objects, produced primarily for the kitchen, could withstand high heat and often went from the stove to the table. Originally developed at the end of the eighteenth century in Scotland and England—the Derbyshire and Yorkshire areas in particular—yellowware was being produced in America by the turn of the nineteenth century, and by midcentury it was a flourishing cottage industry. With its natural clay deposits, New Jersey was an early center. There also were important potters in Kentucky, Pennsylvania, and New England.

The introduction of molds and mass production revolutionized the output of yellowware. England exported huge quantities until the 1870s, when gas-fired kilns increased American production, causing a sharp decline in English imports. Larger, more automated factories were able to produce a wide variety of wares that were described in and sold through catalogs. From the mid-1860s to the mid-1880s, many of the bigger potteries were concentrated in Ohio, especially in Roseville, East Liverpool, Cincinnati, and later Crooksville. English potters had emigrated to the Midwest, and their experience, along with the area's abundant clay deposits, helped the factories to thrive.

Plain and unadorned at first, molded yellowware bowls, baking dishes, casseroles, cups, and pitchers were soon being decorated with bands of color, and eventually with mochalike and sponged designs. By the end of the nineteenth century embossed motifs were also popular, appearing on batter bowls, canisters, plates, and cookie jars.

Bowls and nappies—round, shallow cooking and serving dishes with flat bottoms and sloped sides—were available in nesting sets, from 3 to 18 inches (7.6 to 45.7 cm) in diameter. The smallest and largest sizes were the most difficult to make.

Many potteries continued to produce yellowware well into the twentieth century. The mass production and durability of yellowware objects make them relatively easy to find to this day. Basic and simple in shape, design, and function, yellowware can easily be integrated into any type of kitchen, from country to high-tech.

LEFT Molded yellowware teapots, all from the turn of the century, were often embossed with a variety of motifs, including flowers and basket-weave designs.

Made by hundreds of individuals and potteries, bowls were the most common form of yellowware and became the basic element of the nineteenth-century American kitchen. Either thrown, molded, or—by the end of the nineteenth century—pressed, the bowls were often decorated with colored bands. Originally they were available in sets from 3 or 4 inches (7.6 or 10.2 cm) up to 18 inches (45.7 cm) in diameter. Early hand-turned bowls tended to be plain, with no surface decorations, bases, or turned lips. Molds appeared about 1830, and after 1860 many bowls were made with turned lips and bases.

ABOVE From the 1920s to the 1940s Brush-McCoy was one of the important American makers of green-glazed mixing bowls, embossed with a variety of geometric motifs.

RIGHT Sets of molded yellowware bowls with green glaze in graduated sizes were made in the American Midwest between 1900 and 1930.

LEFT Matched sets of containers, called canister sets, were used to store pantry staples such as rice and cereal, as well as spices, and were a yellowware production basic for many decades. The number and variety of these kitchen pieces grew to include bread bins, rolling pins, butter crocks, and salt boxes. Brush-McCoy was the manufacturer of the banded set, which was produced during World War I. Hull produced the embossed set.

BELOW Yellowware pitchers with banded decorations were available in a wide variety of sizes, from tiny creamers to large ewers. Whether they were thrown or cast, they usually had applied handles and spouts.

Lipped batter bowls in graduated sizes, nesting pie plates, and nappie dishes, some dating from the second half of the nineteenth century, can still be put to good use today. Although quite plain-looking and primitive in feeling, the pottery fits in nicely in a 1940s vintage kitchen, a look that happens to be back in style.

LEFT Rockingham is a kind of yellowware that is dipped in a clear glaze and then covered with a dark brown manganese glaze applied in a spatterwarelike manner. Pie plates, bean pots, batter bowls, molds, platters, and pipkins—small earthenware cooking pots—were available and made in quantity in the early twentieth century. Often, baking dishes went from the oven directly to the table.

RIGHT Oval, round, or rectangular in shape, yellowware molds often featured figurative details, such as fish, rabbits, or ears of corn, which sometimes made allusions to the puddings, blancmanges, and potted meats and fish prepared in them.

OVERLEAF A green-glazed pitcher with a wood-grain design and a molded green bowl are integrated into the decor of a contemporary country kitchen.

ABOVE AND RIGHT Some yellowware pitchers and bowls have distinctive mocha dendritic, seaweed-band, or earthworm—which the potters of the period called cable—decorations. The bands of solid color accentuate the softer, contrasting designs. Pitchers and bowls like these were made in England and the United States between 1860 and 1880.

DIRECTORY

F lea markets have for years been the places to look for all kinds of kitchen ceramics. More recently, however, as older, high-quality pieces have become rarer, dealers have started specializing in one or more kinds of pottery. Listed below are dealers in the United States, France, England, Ireland, the Philippines, and Portugal who have proven to be good sources for one or more types of wares and often have helped collectors build their own enviable collections.

UNITED STATES

Mary and Bill Arciprete
COUNTRY KITCHEN ANTIQUES
Huntington, N.Y.
(516) 271-2238
Spongeware

THE ARTIQUE AT SANDPIPER ANTIQUES
1524 South Broadway
Denver, Colo. 80210
(303) 777-4384
Yellowware

BLUEBIRD ANTIQUES
4 South Main Street
Mayville, Wis. 53050
(414) 387-5711
Yellowware

Nancy S. Boyd
ANTIQUE SHOP
2466 Main Street
Bridgehampton, N.Y.
Mailing address: 25 Mill Hill Lane
East Hampton, N.Y. 11937
(516) 329-3241
Spongeware

T. BROWN AMERICAN ANTIQUES
710 Waterdam Road
McMurray, Penn. 15317
(412) 941-7143
Spongeware

CAMPBELL HOUSE ANTIQUES
805 William Street
Baltimore, Md. 21230
(410) 752-7653
Mochaware

CANTERBURY HOUSE ANTIQUES
1776 Canterbury Street
Jacksonville, Fla. 32205
(904) 387-1776
Yellowware, blue-and-white spongeware

COUNTRY TREASURES
3531 West Springfield Drive
Florence, S.C. 29501
(803) 669-3363
Yellowware, mochaware

Ernest and Beverly Dieringer
DIERINGER'S ARTS & ANTIQUES
75 Sport Hill Road
West Redding, Conn.
Mailing address: P.O. Box 536
Redding Ridge, Conn. 06876
White ironstone
Contact mailing address for
White Ironstone China
Association, Inc., newsletter

GREG ELLINGTON
Wilmington, Ohio 45177
(513) 382-4311
Yellowware, blue-and-white spongeware

RUFUS FOSHEE ANTIQUES
Route 1 (3 1/2 miles north of
   Village Green)
Mailing address: Box 839
Camden, Maine 04843
(207) 236-2838
Spongeware

JOHN AND LYNN GALLO ANTIQUES
75 Main Street
Otego, N.Y. 13825
(607) 988-9963
Yellowware

Sidney Gecker
AMERICAN FOLK ART
226 West 21st Street
New York, N.Y. 10011
(212) 929-8769
Redware

LEFT Behind a screen door, new ironstone dishes and bowls are stored on the pantry shelves of a Long Island country house.

CH

GERANIUM ANTIQUES
P.O. Box 278
Dorset, Vt. 05251
(802) 867-5588
Mochaware, spongeware

GROSBEAK ANTIQUES
Alpharetta, Ga. 30202
(404) 740-8553
Redware

GLORIA G. HAGADONE ANTIQUES
2609 Kimbrough Circle
Charlottesville, Va. 22901
(804) 293-1111
Ironstone

Jeffrey Beal Henkel
HKH INCORPORATED
277 Dodds Lane
Princeton, N.J. 08540
(609) 921-2527
Ironstone

Robert E. Kinnaman
BRIAN A. RAMAEKERS INC.
2466 Main Street
Bridgehampton, N.Y. 11932
Mailing address: Box 1140
Wainscott, N.Y. 11975
(516) 537-0779
Mochaware

Nancy Knudsen
QUILTS & COUNTRY ANTIQUES
Orange, Conn.
(203) 795-0335
Spongeware

Nancy and Dan Kosiewski
FEATHER TREE ANTIQUES
54 Redstone Hill
Lancaster, Mass. 01523
(508) 365-6456
Yellowware, stoneware

LYNWOOD'S OF LIVINGSTON
COUNTY
Pontiac, Ill. 61764
(815) 842-1687
Spongeware

George and Carol Meekins
COUNTRY TREASURES
Main Street
Mailing address: P.O. Box 277
Preston, MD 21655
(410) 673-2603
Yellowware

PRIMITIVES
P.O. Box 202
Asheboro, N.C. 27203
(910) 625-2962
Spongeware, mochaware

JONATHAN RICKARD
73 North Main Street
Deep River, Conn. 06417
(860) 526-3562
Mochaware

LEWIS W. SCRANTON ANTIQUES
224 Roast Meat Hill
Killingworth, Conn. 06419
(860) 663-1060
New England redware, stoneware

FREDERIC I. THALER
Cornwall Bridge, Conn. 06754
(203) 672-0052
Ironstone

INGRID TRAUGOTT ANTIQUES
37006 East State Road 2
Garden City, Mo. 64747-9729
Ironstone

Richard and Carolyn F. Weeks
WEEKS ANTIQUES
RFD 5, Box 2489
Cundy's Harbor
Brunswick, Maine 04011
(207) 725-4772
*Yellowware, blue-and-white
spongeware, mochaware*

Elizabeth Zwicker
BRISTOL BARN ANTIQUES
Route 130
Bristol, Maine 04539
(207) 563-3897
Spongeware

ENGLAND

GARRY ATKINS
107 Kensington Church Street
London W8 7LN
0171 727-8737
Early mochaware, spongeware

CEDAR ANTIQUES
High Street
Hartley Wintney
Hampshire
01252 843-252
Mochaware

JONATHAN HORNE
ANTIQUES LIMITED
66C Kensington Church Street
London W8 4BY
0171 221-5658
Fax: 0171 792-3090
Spongeware

VALERIE HOWERD
2 Campden Street
London W8 7EP
0171 972-9702
Ironstone

THE LACQUER CHEST
75 Kensington Church Street
London W8 4BG
0171 937-1306
Mochaware

OLD RECTORY FARM ANTIQUES
Great Fransham between
    Swaffham and Dereham,
    just off the A47
01362 687-206
*Ironstone, spongeware, mochaware,
redware*

LH

ANNA WOLSEY LIBRA ANTIQUES
131D Kensington Church Street
London W8 7PT
0171 727-2990
Mochaware

IRELAND

BYGONES OF IRELAND
John van Wensveen
Westport-Castlebar Road
County Mayo
098 26132

HONAN'S ANTIQUES
Crowe Street, Gort
County Clare
and
O'Conell Street, Ennis
County Clare
091 631407

VICTOR MITCHELL
Mount Butler
Roscrea
05 21 396

ROS SHAW
Belfast
Northern Ireland
01232 710-119
Spongeware

FRANCE

AUTREFOIS
10, rue Ernest-Cresson
75014 Paris
01 45 40 61 63

BACHELIER ANTIQUITÉS
Marché Paul Bert
18, rue Paul Bert
93400 Saint-Ouen
01 40 11 89 98

LES DEUX ORPHELINES
21, place des Vosges
75004 Paris
01 42 72 63 87

FANETTE
1, rue d'Alençon
75015 Paris
01 42 22 21 73

AU FOND DE LA COUR
49, rue de Seine
75006 Paris
01 43 25 81 89

LA GALERIE PITTORESQUE
Le Louvre des Antiquaires
2, place du Palais Royal
75001 Paris
01 42 61 58 06

L'IMPREVU
21, rue Guénégaud
75006 Paris
01 43 54 65 09

MARCHÉS AUX PUCES
L'Isle sur la Sorgue (Provence)
    84800 / Sundays
Montreuil (Porte de Paris) 93100 /
    weekends and Mondays
Vanves (Porte de Paris) 92170 /
    Saturdays and Sunday mornings

LA PETITE COUSINE
Christiane Schwartz
78, rue Gay Lussac
75005 Paris
01 43 54 35 89

MICHEL SONKIN
10, rue de Beaune
75007 Paris
01 42 61 27 87

VIVEMENT JEUDI
52, rue Mouffetard
75005 Paris
01 43 31 44 52

PHILIPPINES

TAWALISI ANTIQUES
Lu O. Centre
1000 Makati Ave., corner of
    Amalz Street
Makati
Ueiro Wahila
632 84 41 977

PORTUGAL

FERIA DA LADRA
Campo da Santa Clara
Alfama
Lisbon

GALERIA DA SÉ
Rua Augusto Rosa 46-48
1100 Lisbon
01 886 42 41

MURTEIRA
Rua Augusto Rosa 19-21
1100 Lisbon
01 886 38 51

OUTRA ERA
Largo de Sto-Antonio
    da Sé 14-15-16
1100 Lisbon
01 888 35 05

RUI QUINTELA
Rua da Escola Politécnica 39
1250 Lisbon
01 342 49 64

XIREL
Rua D. Pedro V, 111
1200 Lisbon
01 346 02 66

OVERLEAF Redware bowl and lid, probably made in Lancaster County, Pennsylvania, and meant to be decorative rather than functional. The outer wall of this double-walled piece is decorated with pierced carvings and has twisted-rope handles.

CH

BIBLIOGRAPHY

Brewer, Mary. *Collector's Guide to Rockingham: The Enduring Ware*. Paducah, Ky.: Collector Books, 1996.

Comstock, H.E. *The Pottery of the Shenandoah Valley Region*. Winston-Salem, N.C.: The Museum of Early Southern Decorative Arts, 1994.

Gallo, John. *Nineteenth and Twentieth Century Yellow Ware*. Richfield Springs, N.Y.: Heritage Press, 1985.

Huxford, Sharon and Bob. *The Collectors Encyclopedia of McCoy Pottery*. Paducah, Ky.: Collector Books, 1993.

Ketchum, William C., Jr. *American Country Pottery: Yellowware and Spongeware*. New York: Alfred A. Knopf, 1987.

———. *The Confident Collector: American Pottery and Porcelain Identification and Price Guide*. New York: Avon Books, 1994.

Leibowitz, Joan. *Yellow Ware: The Transitional Ceramic*. West Chester, Pa.: Schiffer Publishing Ltd., 1985.

McAllister, Lisa S., and John L. Michel. *Collecting Yellow Ware: An Identification and Value Guide*. Paducah, Ky.: Collector Books, 1993.

McConnell, Kevin. *Redware: America's Folk Art Pottery*. West Chester, Pa.: Schiffer Publishing Ltd., 1988.

———. *Spongeware and Spatterware*. West Chester, Pa.: Schiffer Publishing Ltd., 1990.

Raycraft, Don and Carol. *Collector's Guide to Country Stoneware and Pottery*. Paducah, Ky.: Collector Books, 1993.

Rickard, Jonathan. "Mochaware." *Antiques* 144, no. 2 (August 1993): 182-89.

Robacker, Earl F. and Ada F. *Spatterware and Sponge: Hardy Perennials of Ceramics*. Cranbury, N.J.: A. S. Barnes and Company, 1978.

Wetherbee, Jean. *A Second Look at White Ironstone*. Lombard, Ill.: Wallace-Homestead Book Company, 1985.

———. *White Ironstone: A Collector's Guide*. Dubuque, Iowa: Antique Trader Books, 1996.

ACKNOWLEDGMENTS

Putting together *Everyday Things™: Kitchen Ceramics* has been an international affair. We would like to thank the European and American collectors and dealers who were so generous in sharing their treasures and letting Marie-Pierre Morel and Marc Schwartz take photographs of them: Jack Anspaugh, Don Carpentier, Ernie and Bev Dieringer, Sydney Gecker, Nancy and Don Kosiewski, Susan and Gerry Lauren, Jean-Louis and Marie-Jeanne Ménard, Tom and Olga Moreland, Marianne Racheline, Jonathan Rickard, and Lewis and Janet Scranton.

Thanks also to Amy Crain, Jane Creech, Willie Frison, Charley Gold and Peri Wolfman, Harry Greenberger, Hélène Maury, Marianne Ménard, Ellen O'Neill, Matt Sarraf, Johnathan Scott, Norma and Tommy Spada, Thomas Woodward and Blanche Greenstein, and Michael, Jake, and Lucie Steinberg.

Because much of the pottery that we have chosen to include in *Everyday Things™: Kitchen Ceramics* was, until quite recently, considered ordinary and unremarkable, we are indebted to the pioneering research that has been done in these fields. Particularly useful were *A Second Look at White Ironstone* by Jean Wetherbee, published in 1985 by the Wallace-Homestead Book Company; *White Ironstone: A Collector's Guide*, a 1996 publication from Antique Trader Books; *Spatterware and Sponge: Hardy Perennials of Ceramics* by Earl F. and Ada F. Robacker, a 1978 book published by A. S. Barns and Company, Inc.; *Spongeware and Spatterware* by Kevin McConnell, published in 1990 by the Schiffer Publishing Company; *Redware: America's Folk Art Pottery* by Kevin McConnell, a 1988 Schiffer Publishing Company book; *The Pottery of the Shenandoah Valley Region* by H. E. Comstock, published in 1994 by the Museum of Early Southern Decorative Arts; and John Gallo's 1988 *Nineteenth and Twentieth Century Yellowware*. Any mistakes or misunderstandings based on these materials are entirely our own.

We would also like to thank our agent, Barbara Hogenson, and our publisher, Abbeville Press: Robert Abrams, Mark Magowan, Patricia Fabricant, Barbara Sturman, and Lou Bilka. We are especially indebted to our two extraordinary editors, Jackie Decter in New York and Marike Gauthier in Paris.

SUZANNE SLESIN, New York
DANIEL ROZENSZTROCH, Paris
STAFFORD CLIFF, London
February 1997

INDEX

Page numbers in *italics* refer to illustrations.

CH

PHOTOGRAPHY CREDITS

City Museum and Art Gallery Stoke on Trent: pp. 14 (bottom), 15, 16, 17; Hulton Getty: p. 18; © Collection Viollet: p. 14 (top).